Cut and Collage: Summer Sunflowers

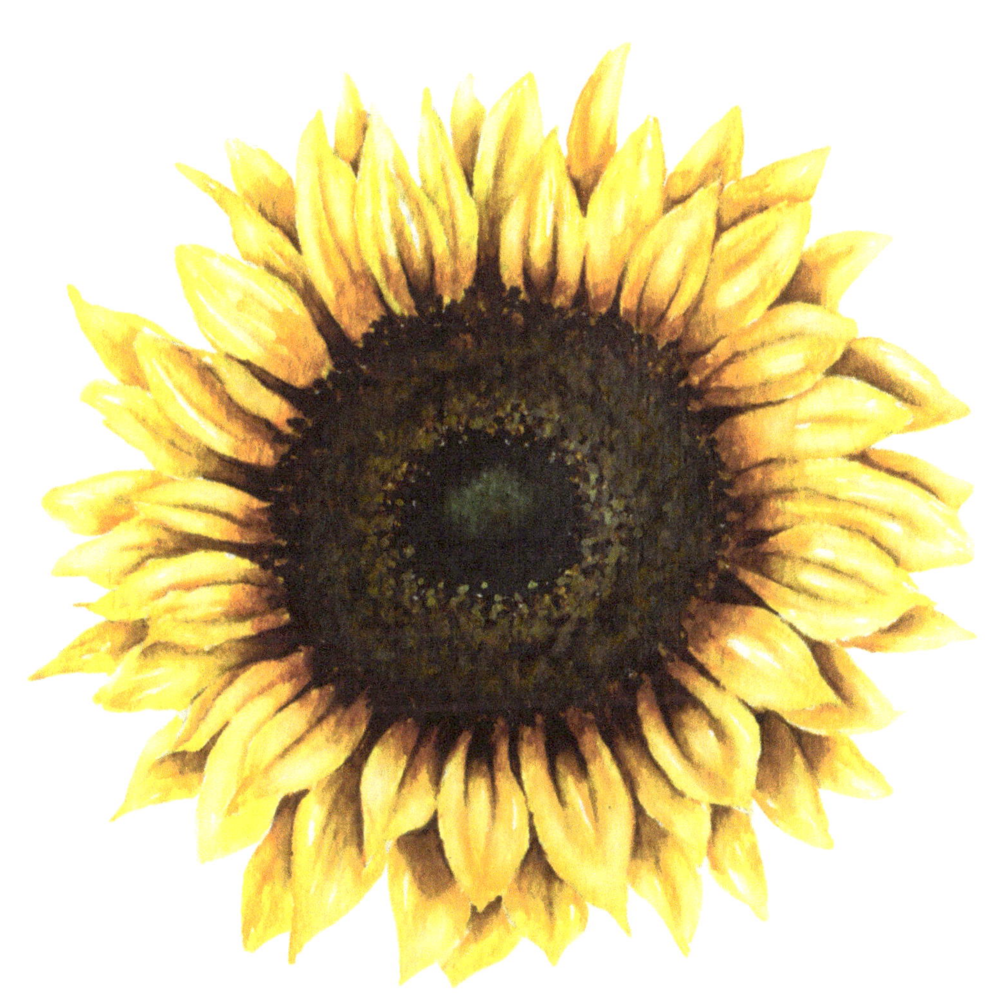

An Art Journaling and Mixed Media Paper Play Book

Welcome to the Art Journaling Paper Play Book! These bright and happy sunflowers will bring a touch of gold to your art, craft and papercrafting projects.

This Book is a Toy!

This book is most definitely a toy. It's for you to cut up, tear apart and play with. Cut out and collage, color, pull out the printed papers and use them in your journal and papercrafts, use the cut-outs to embellish your projects. The patterned papers are perfect for tearing/cutting/collaging into your own creations of all kinds.

Take hold of it and play!

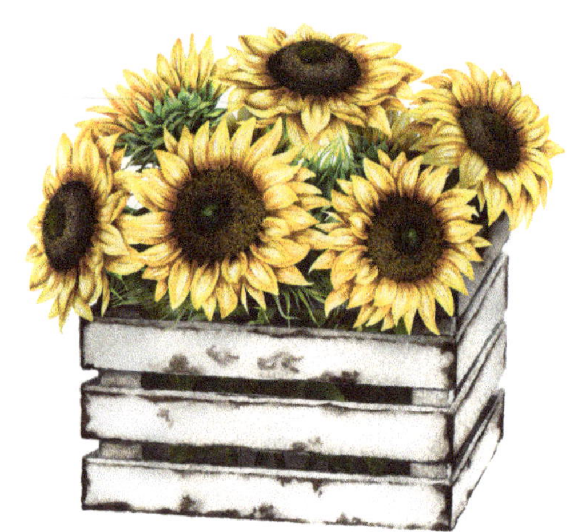

Paperback ISBN: 978-0-9837659-7-4

Published by Tesseray Publishing LLC
7635 148th Street West, #329
Apple Valley, MN 55124
www.TesserayPublishing.com

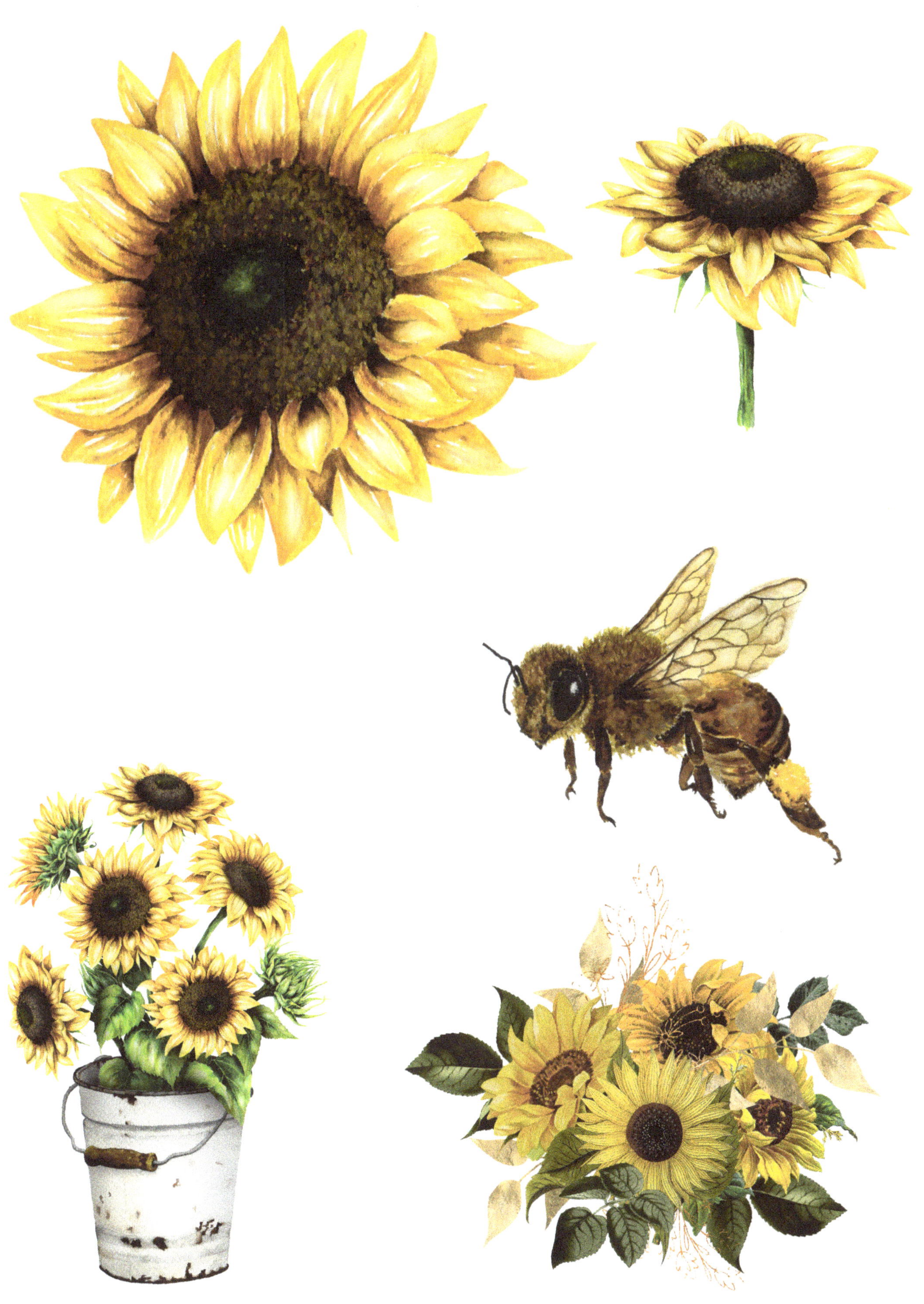

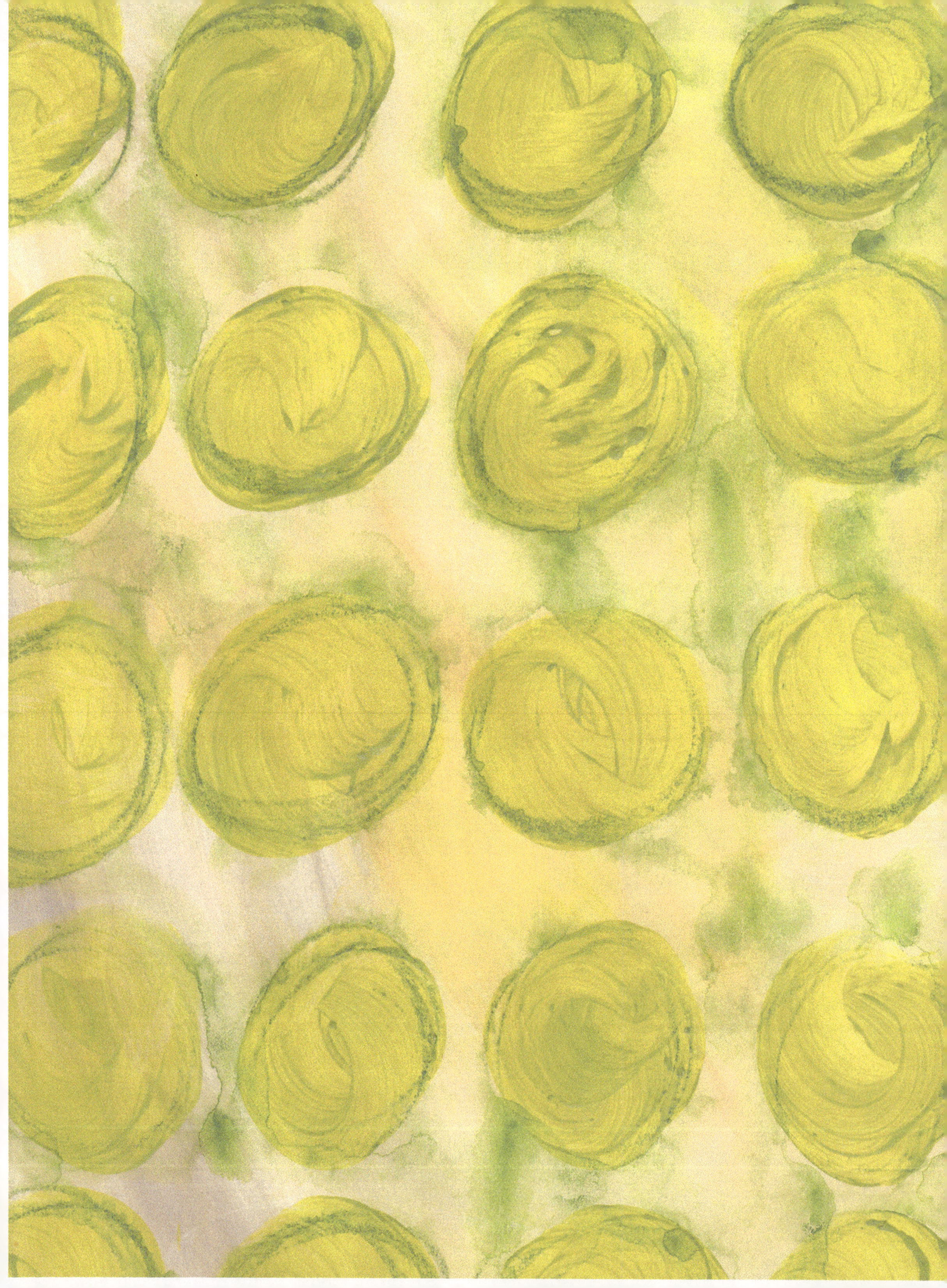

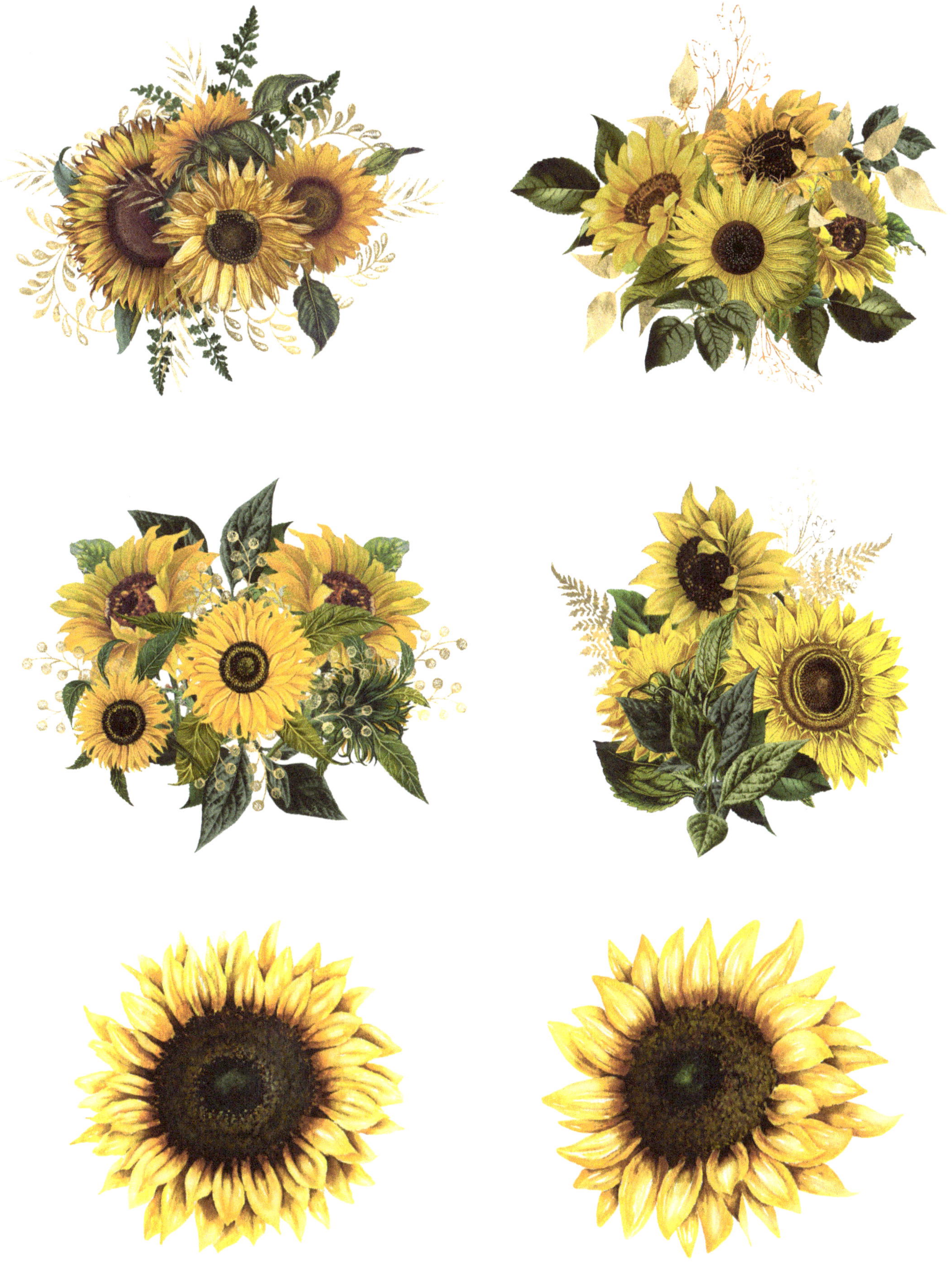

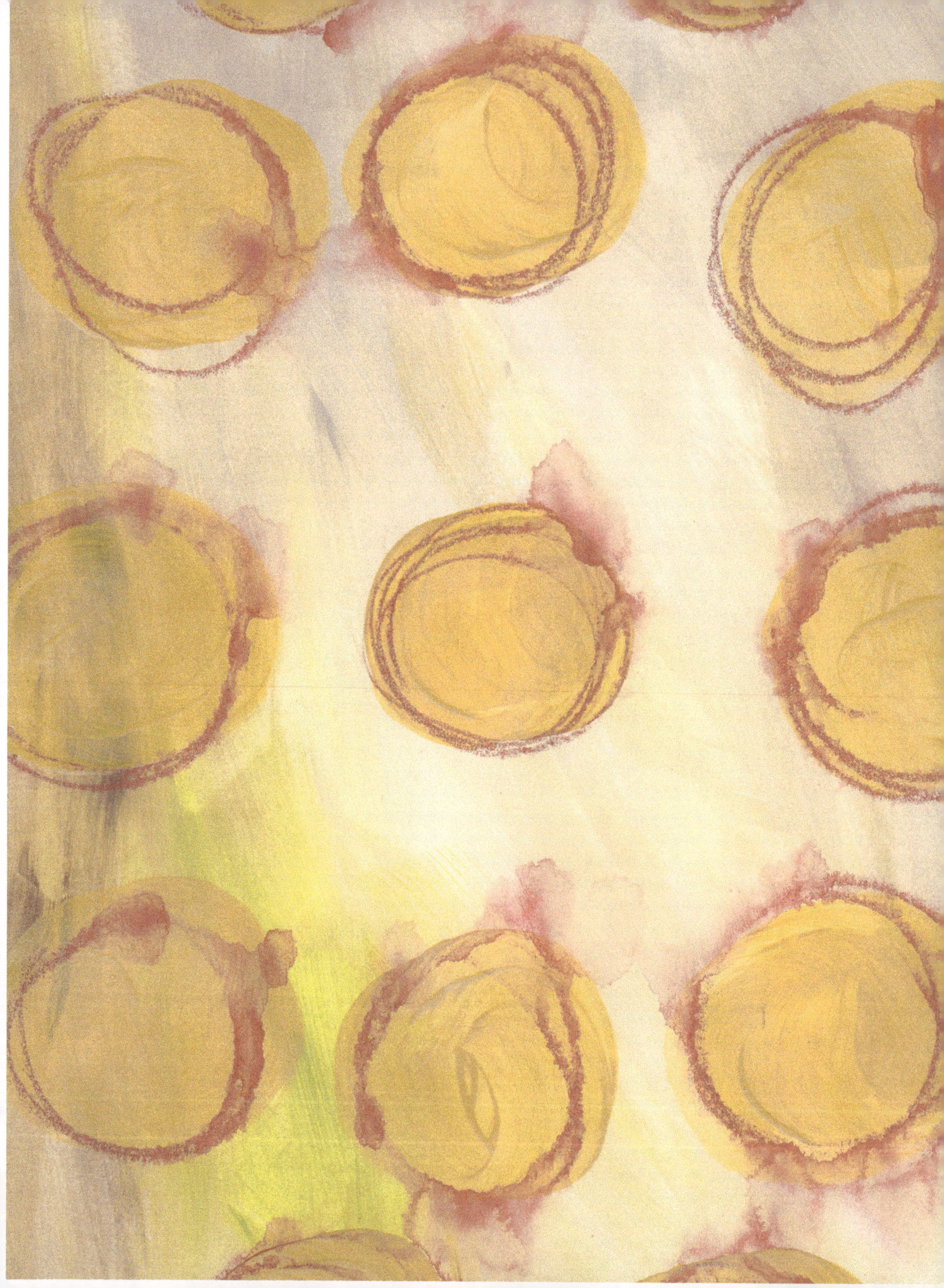

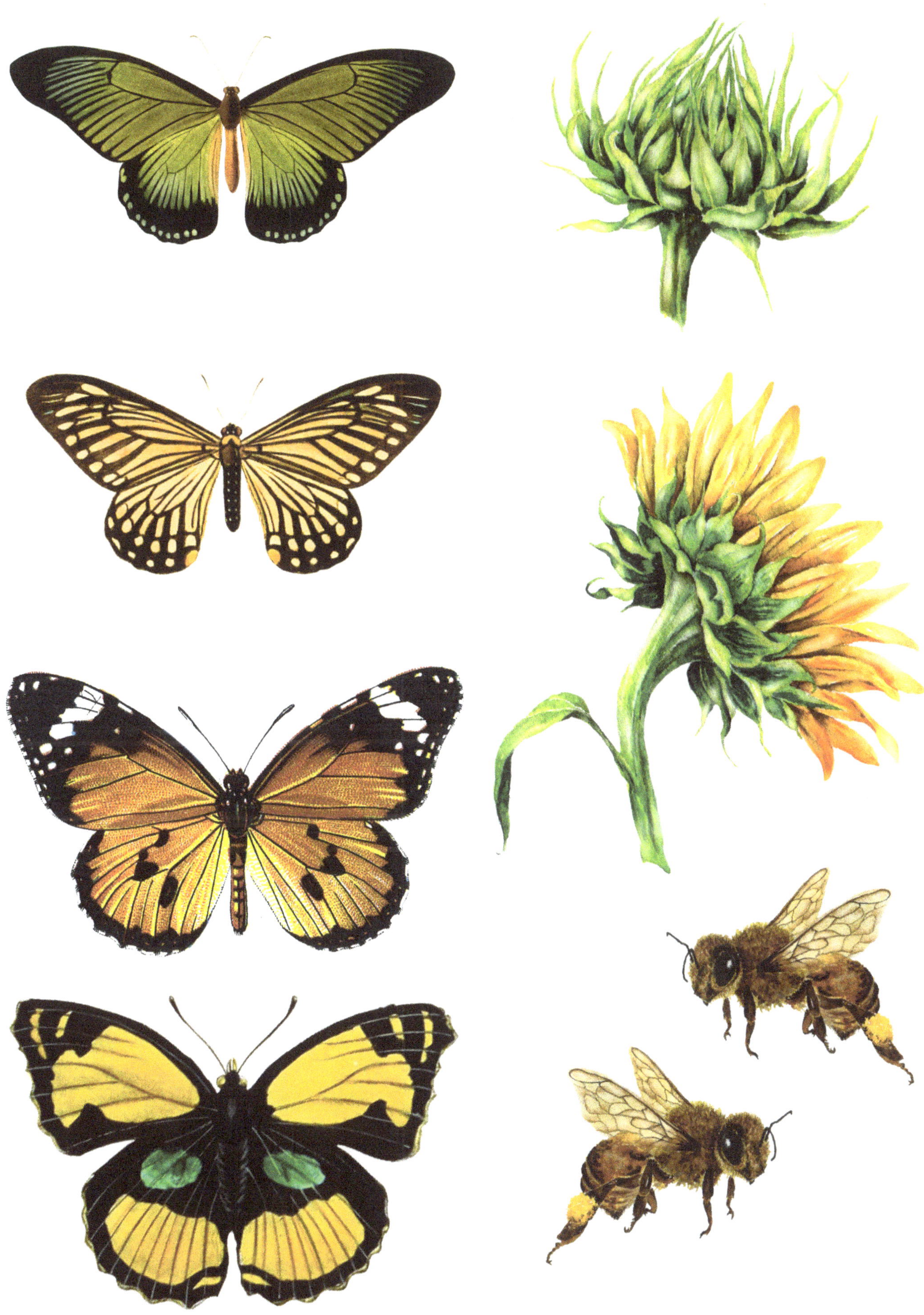

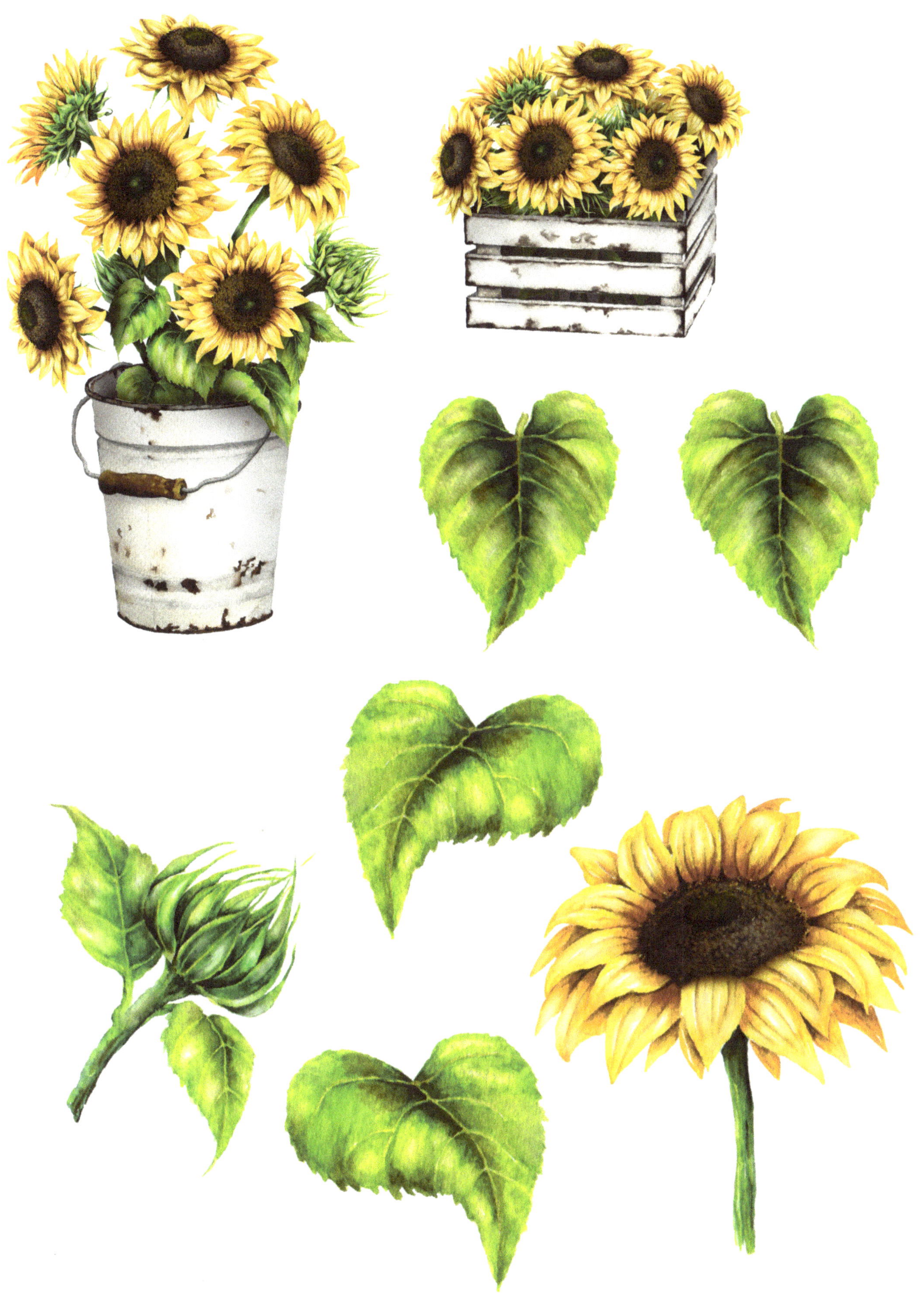

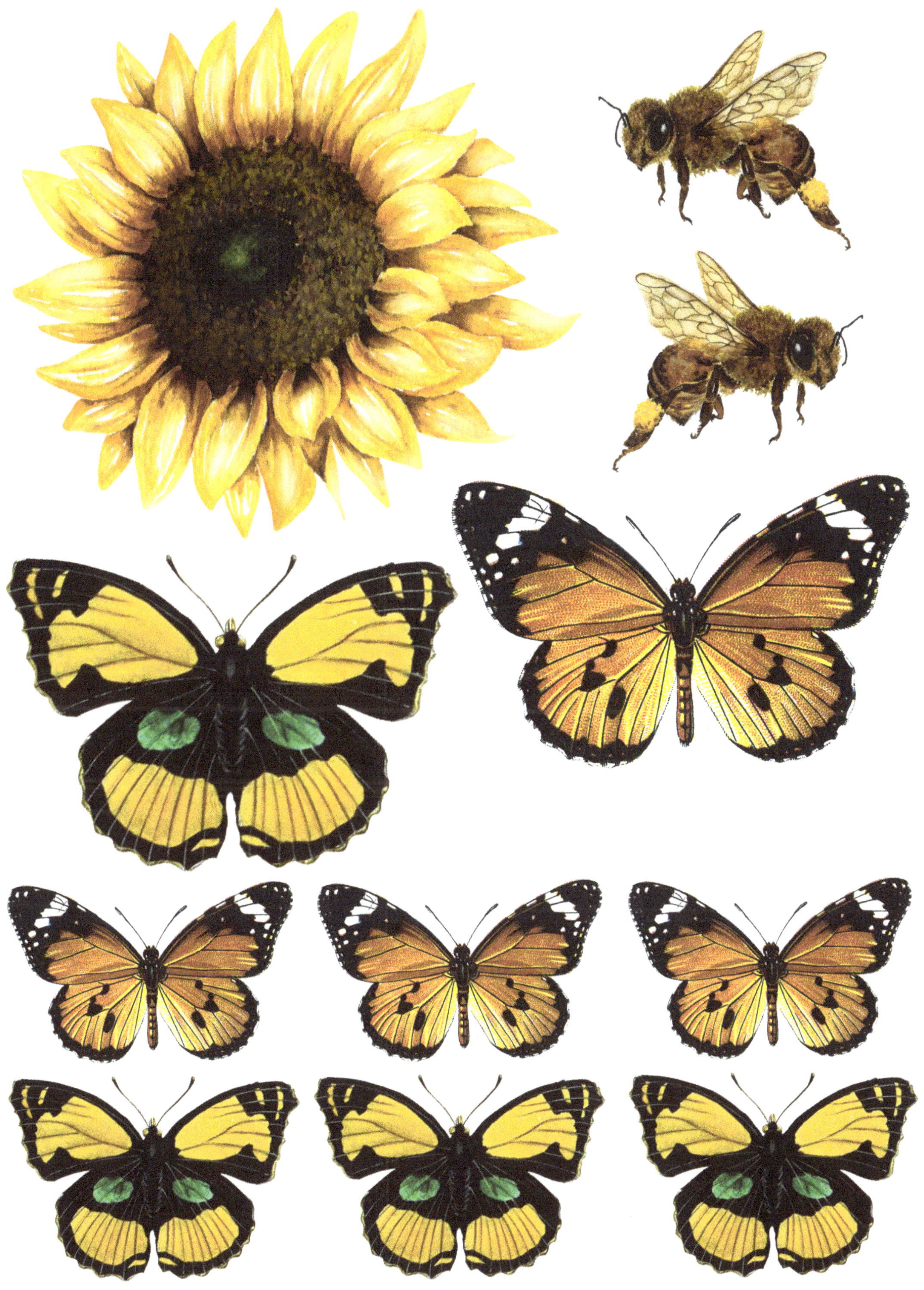

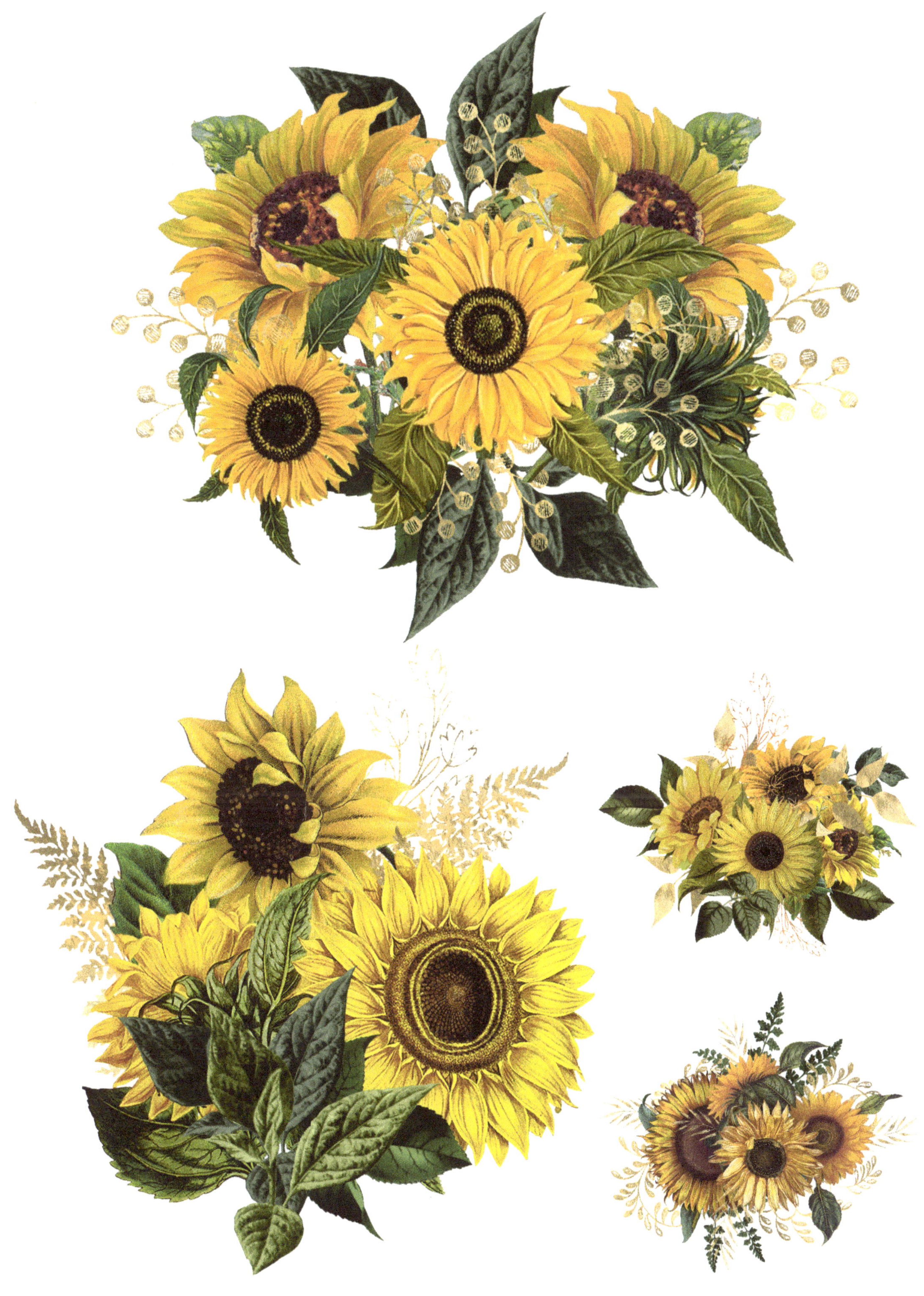

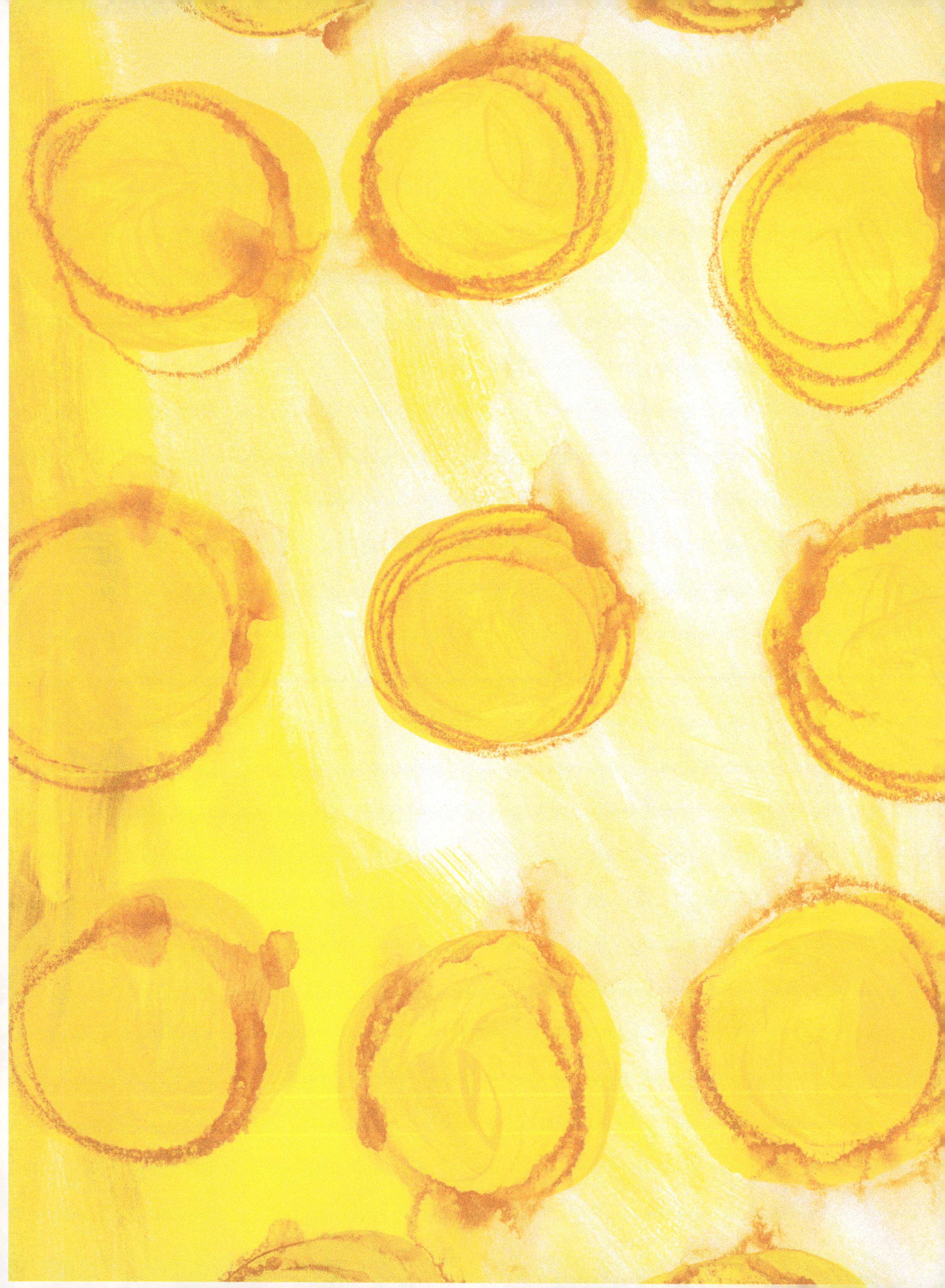

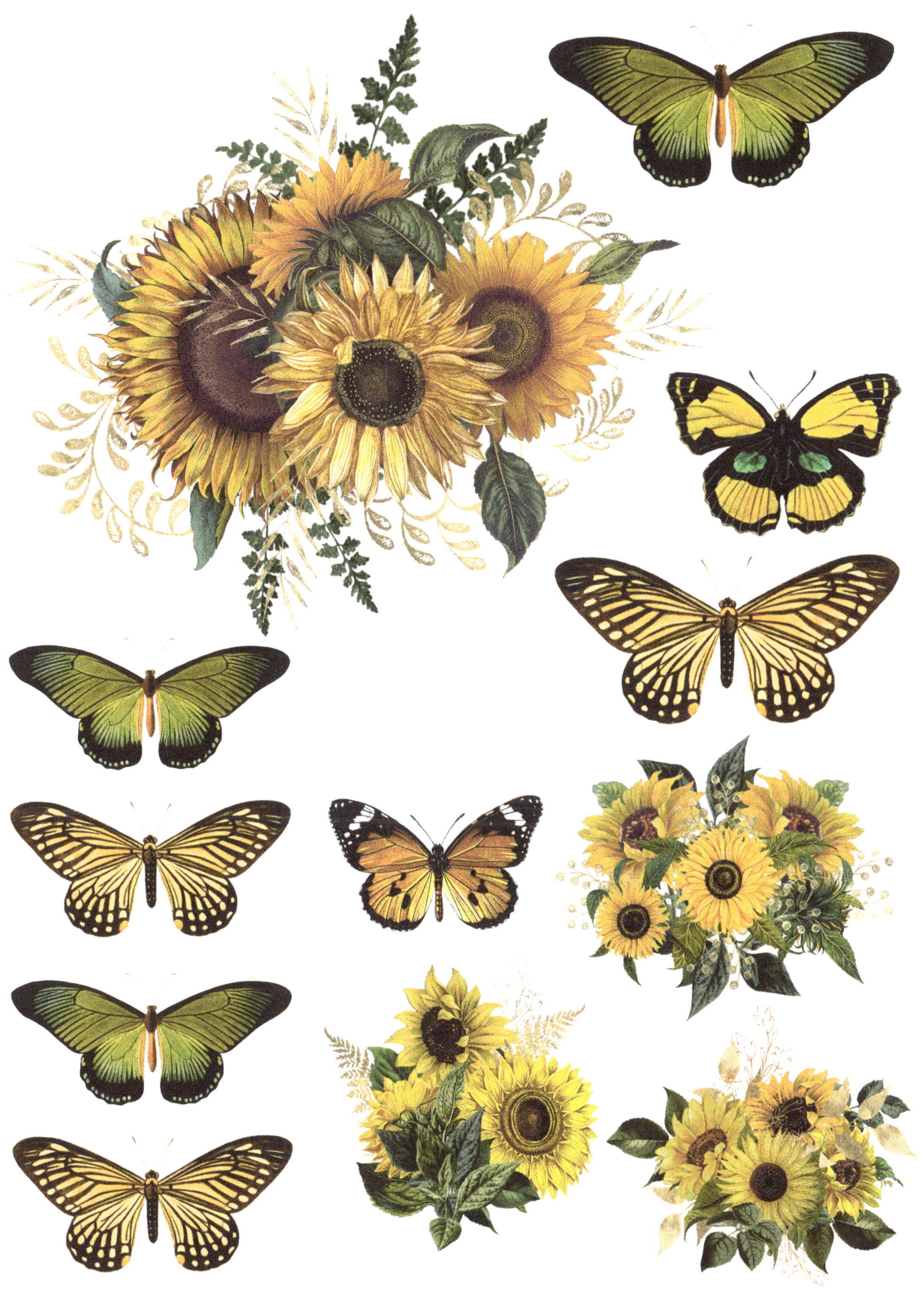

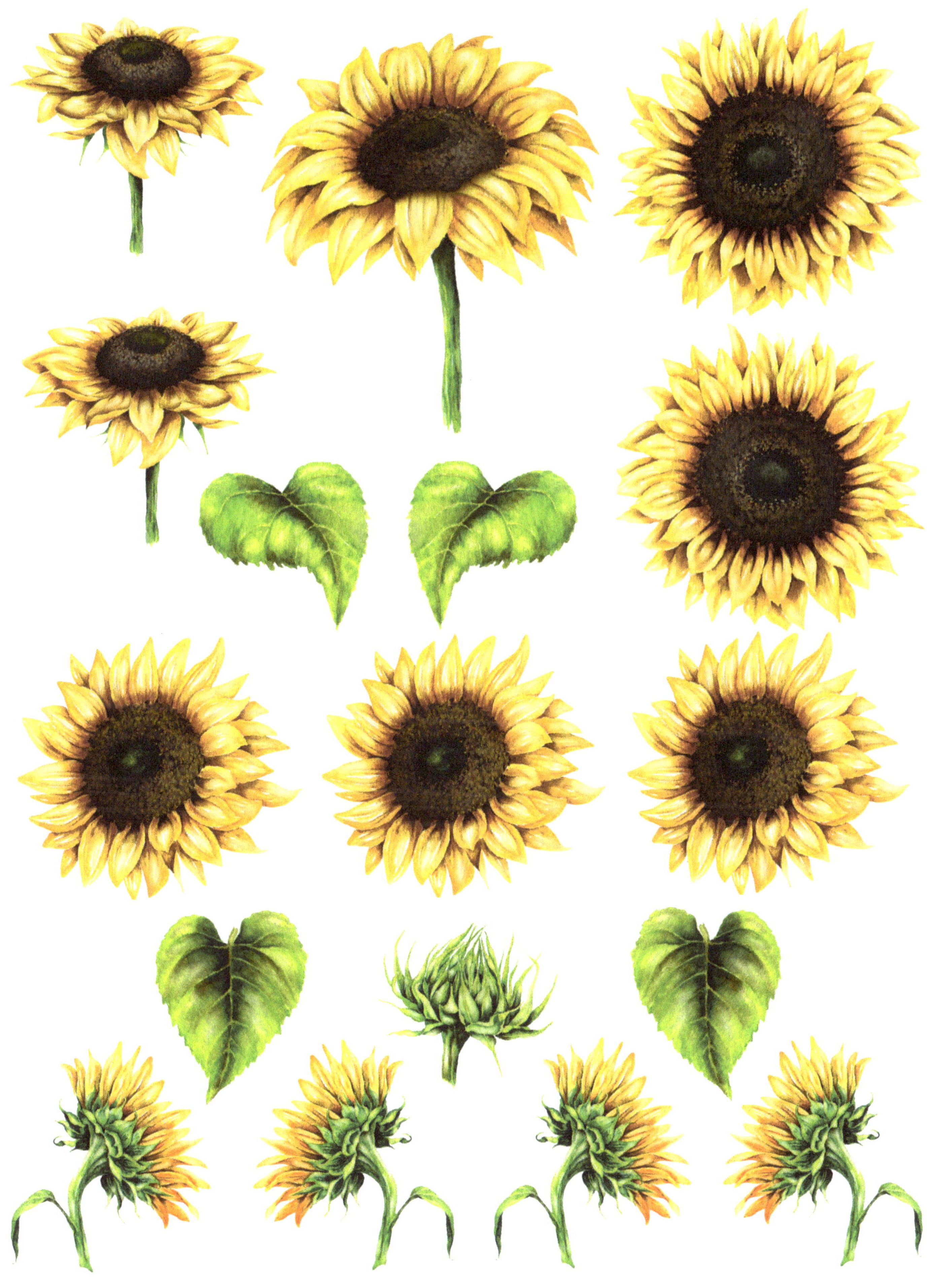

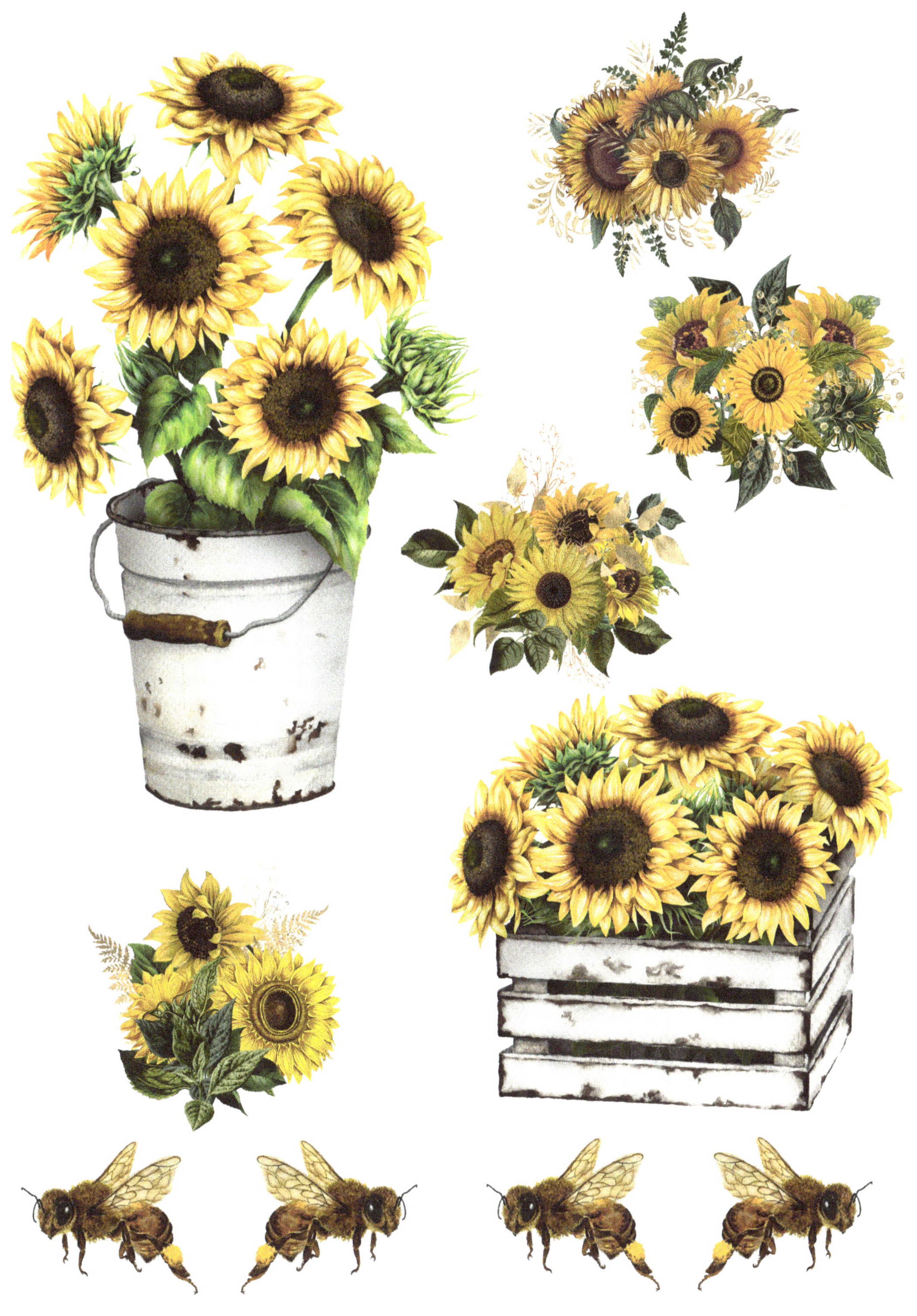

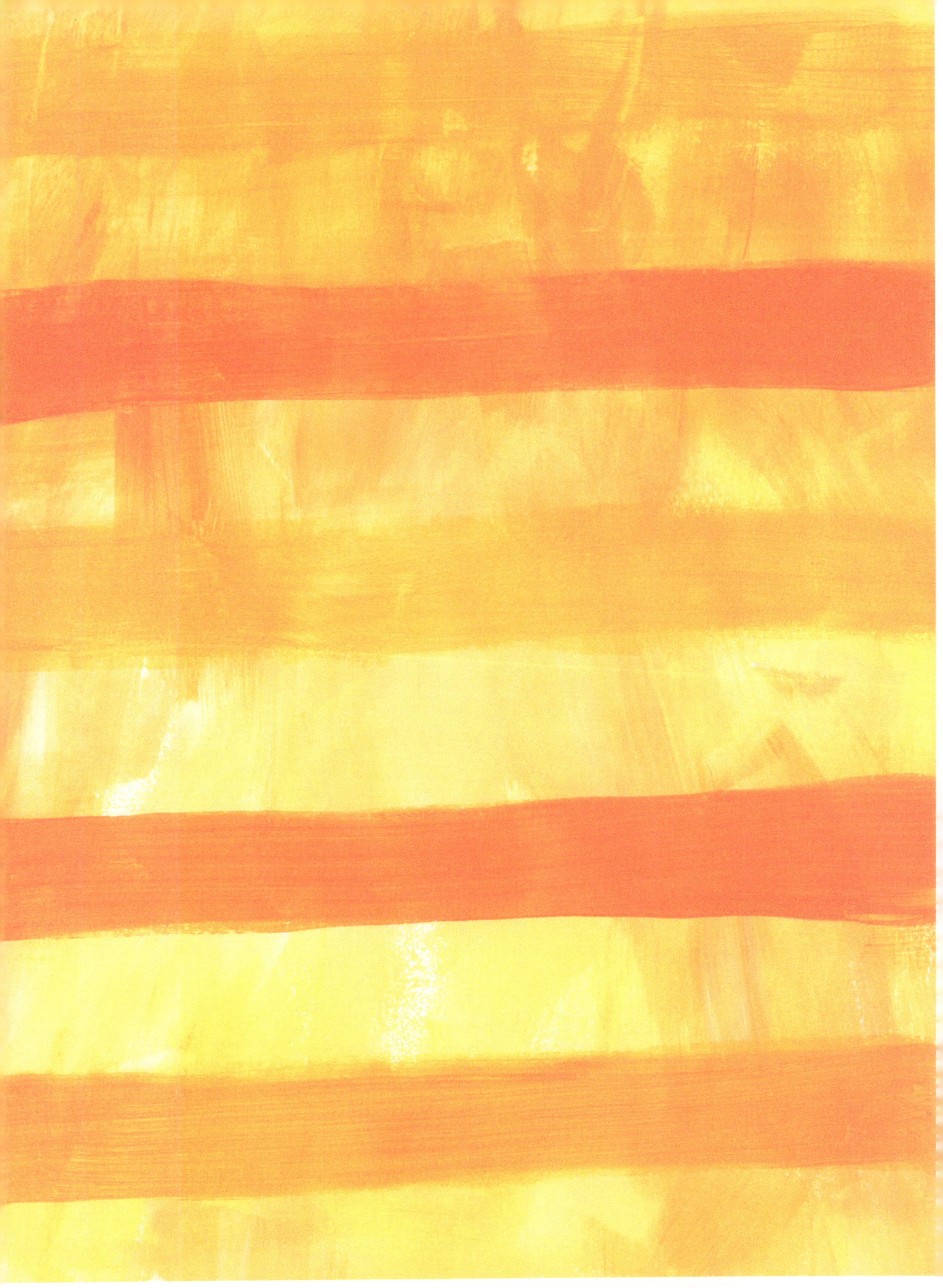

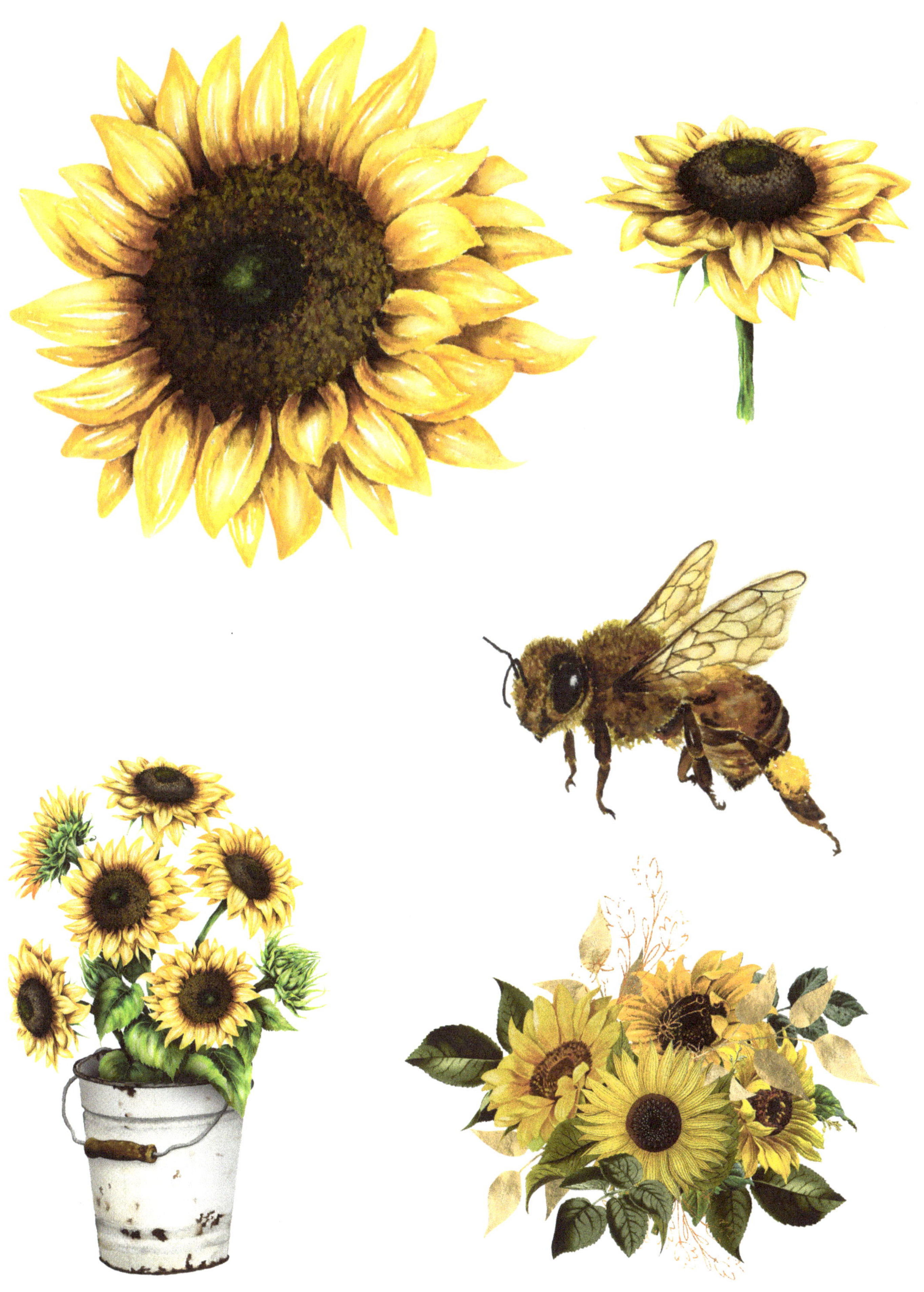

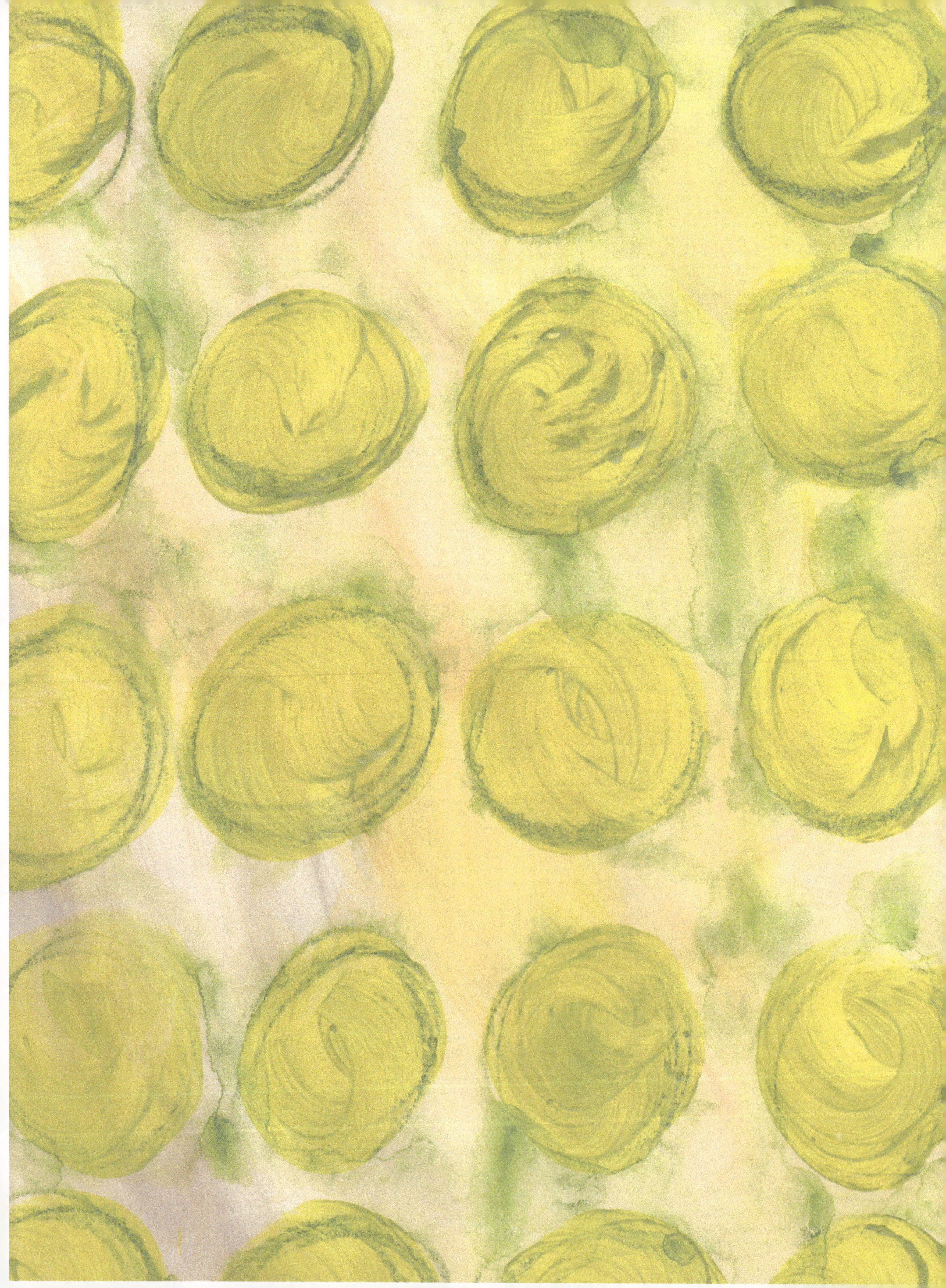

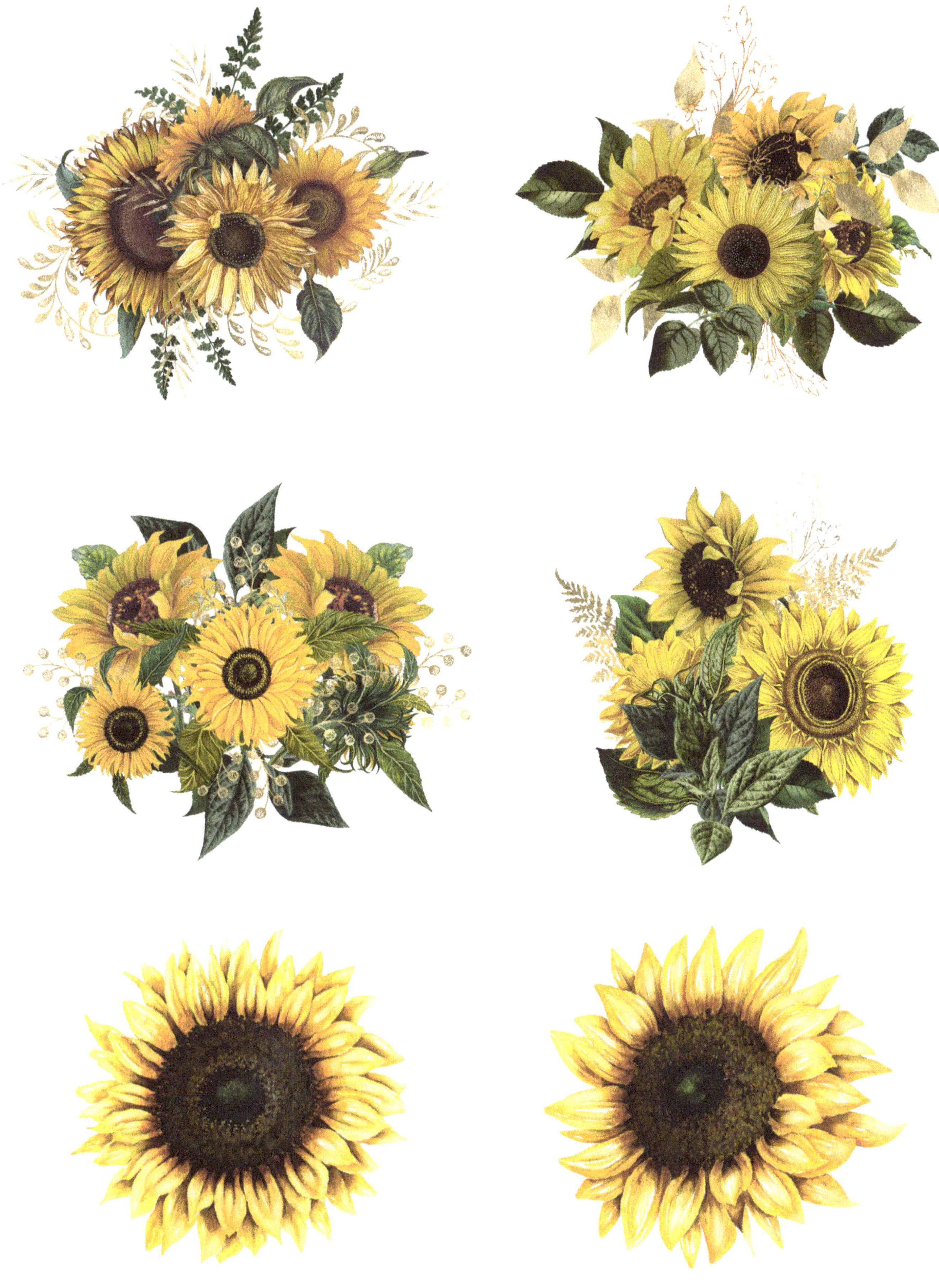

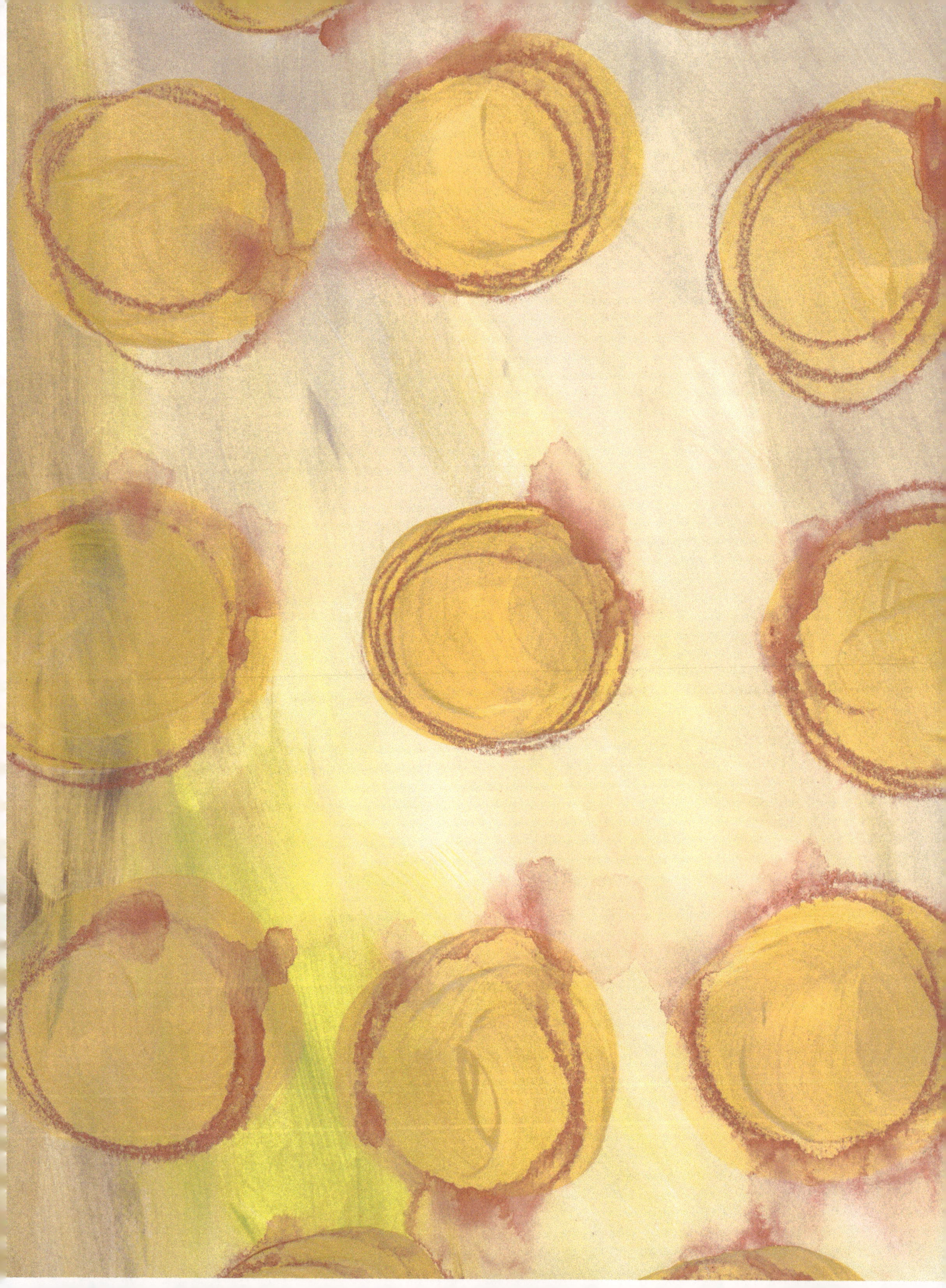

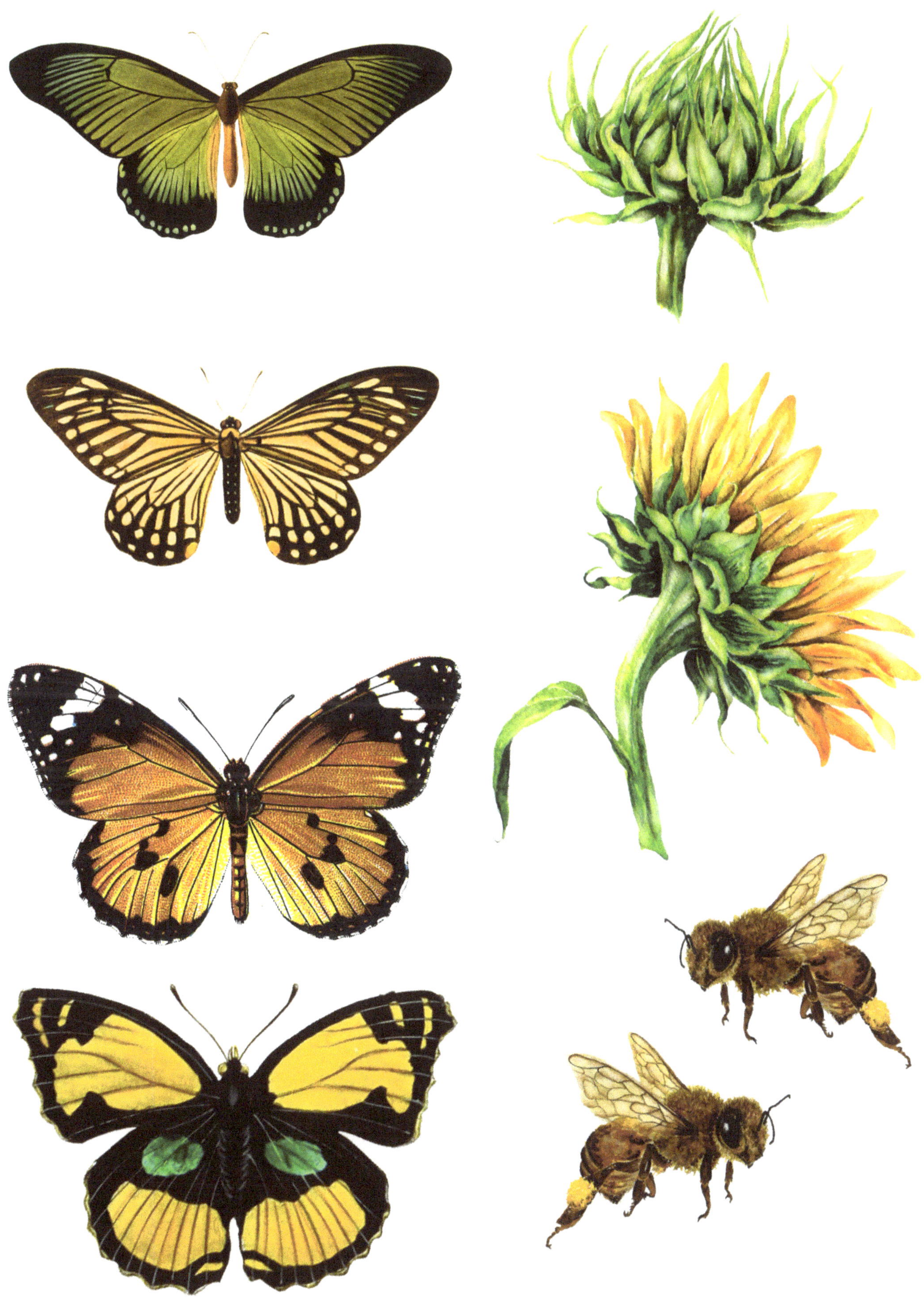

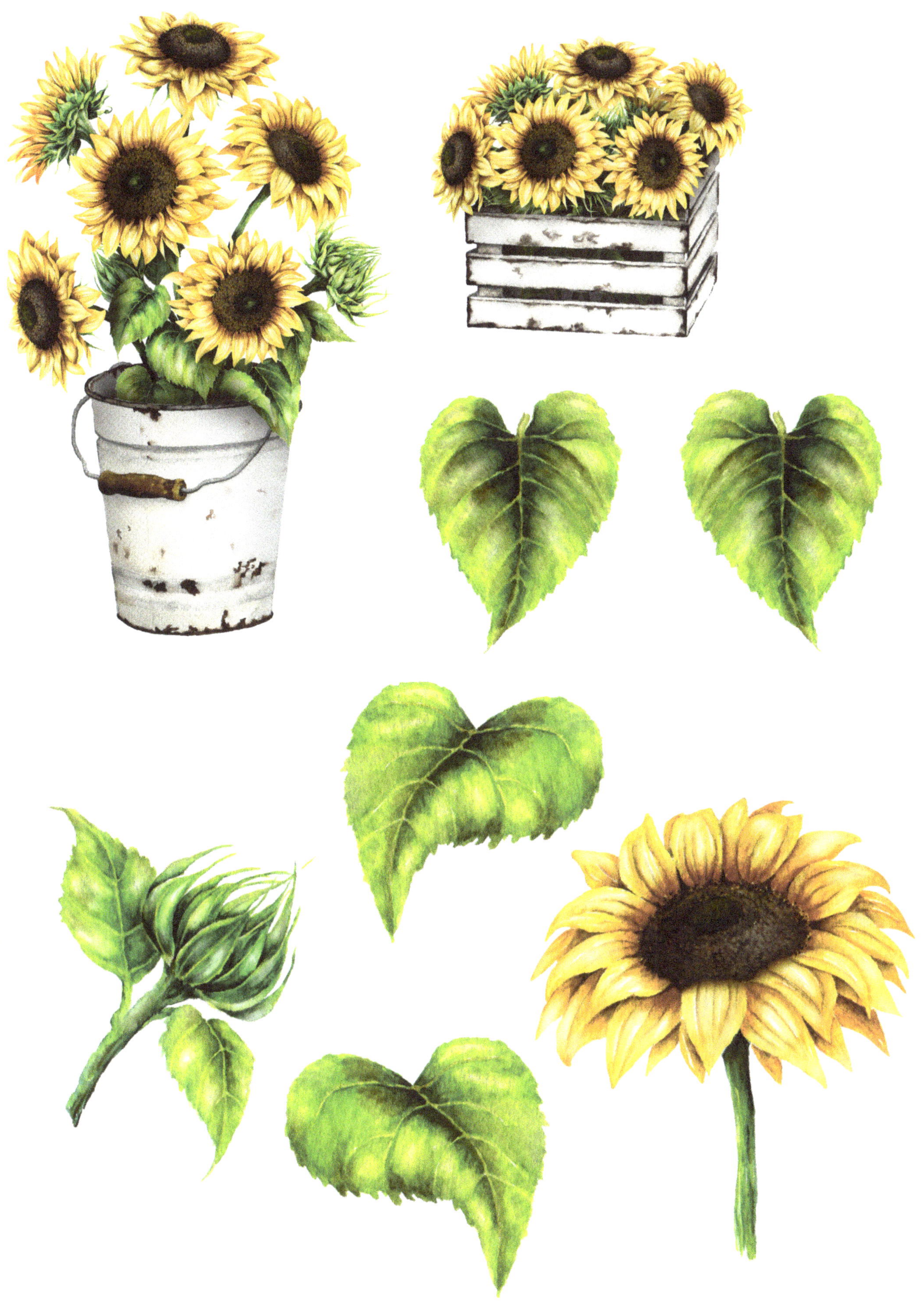

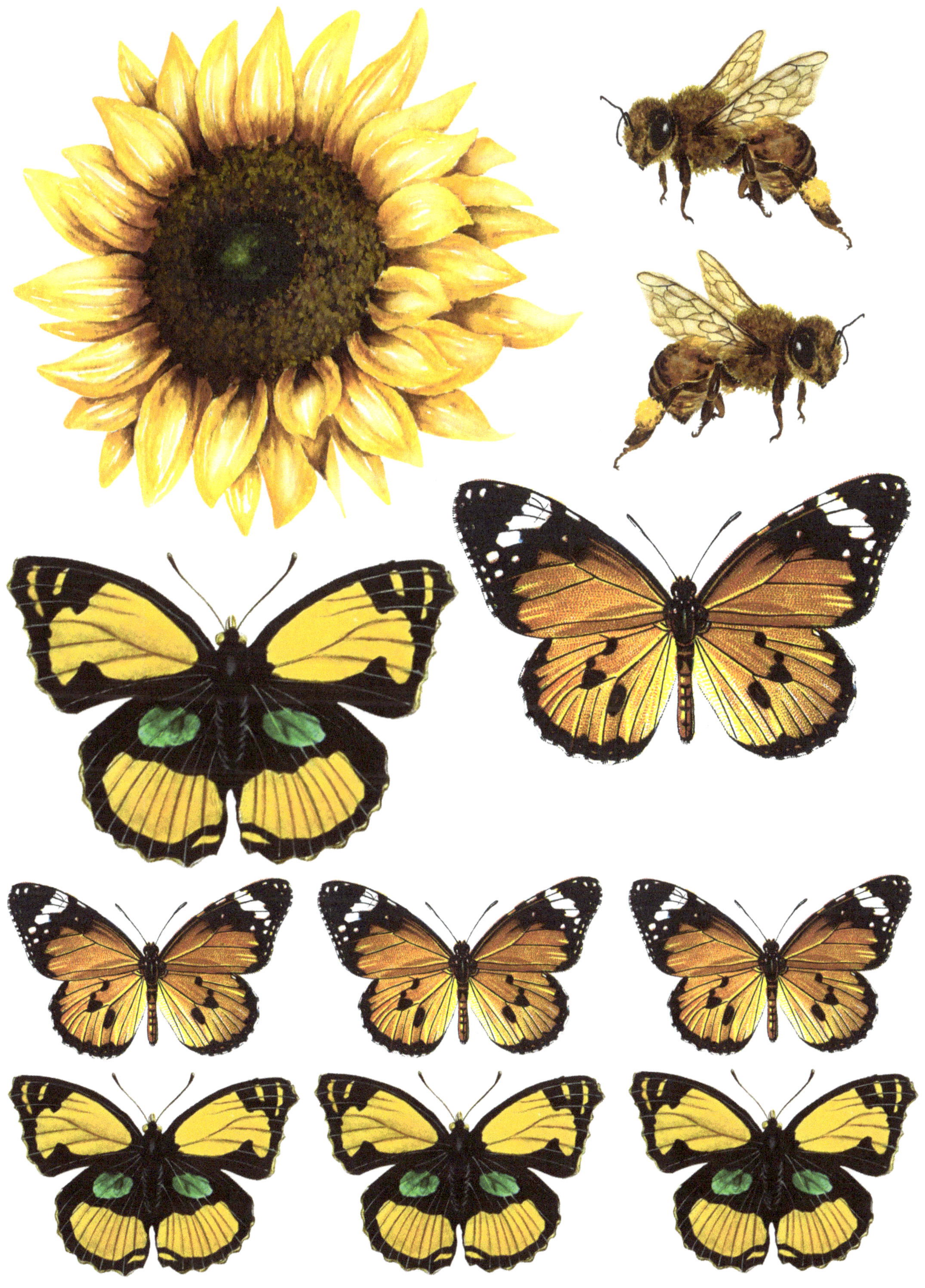

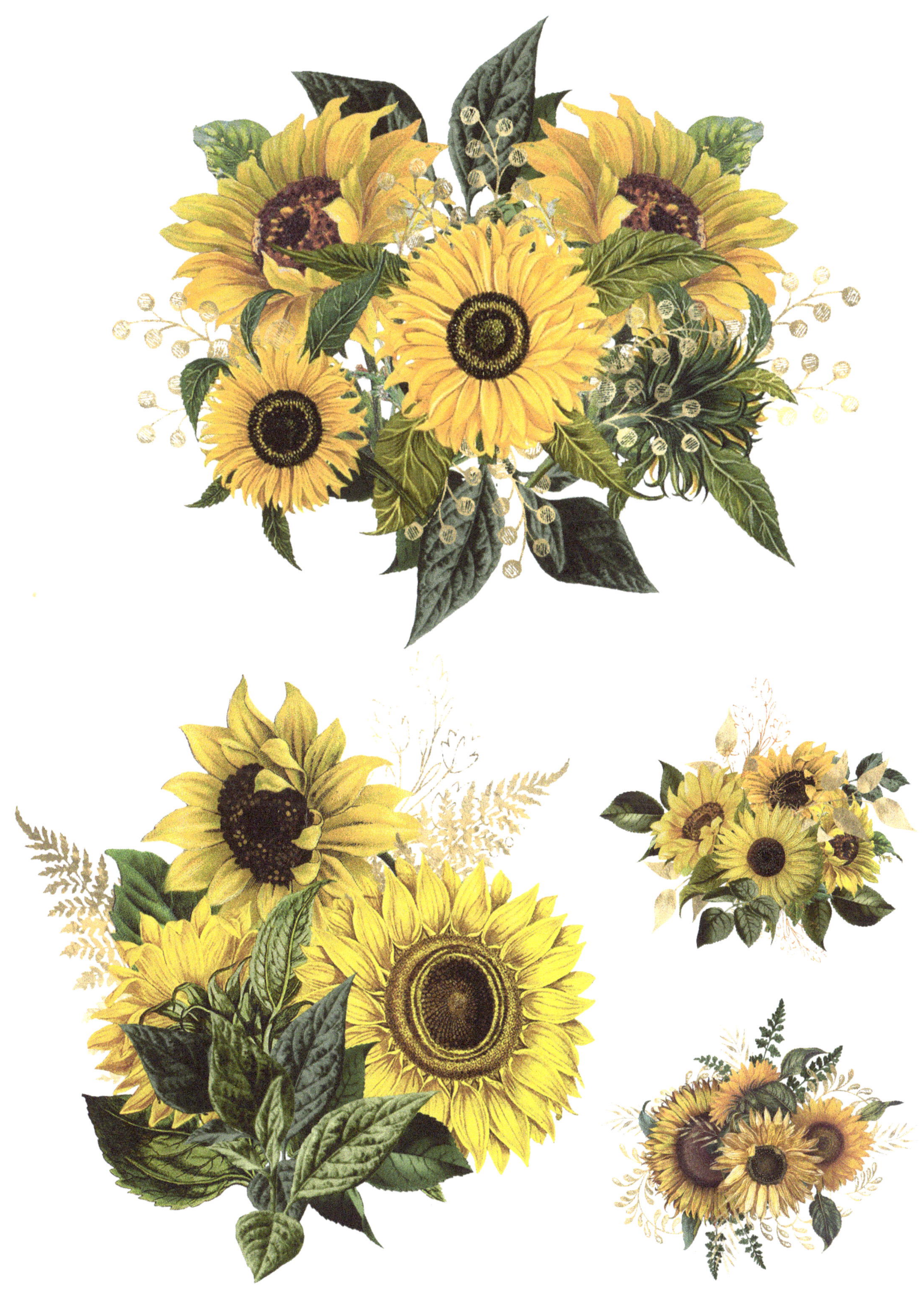

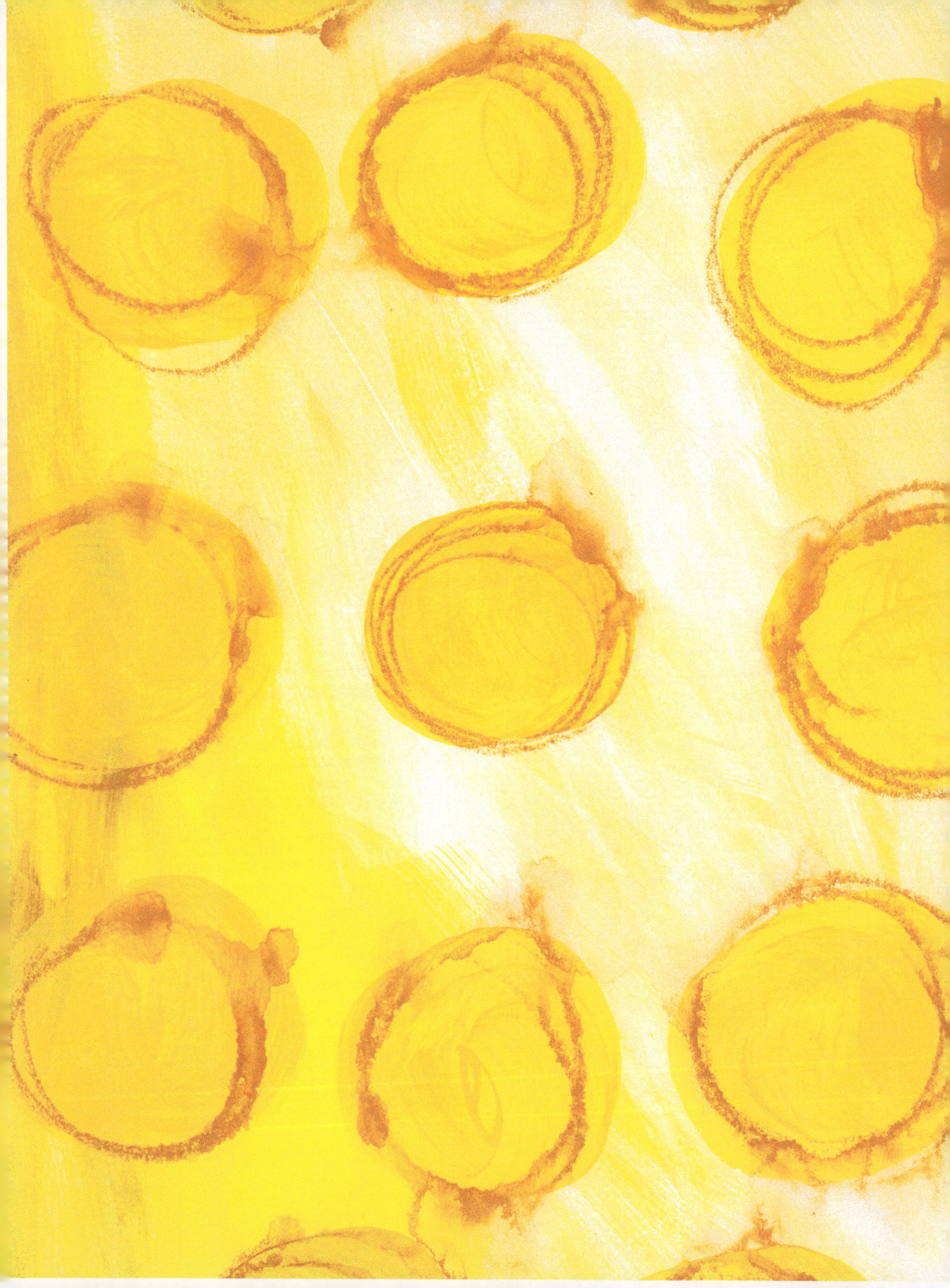

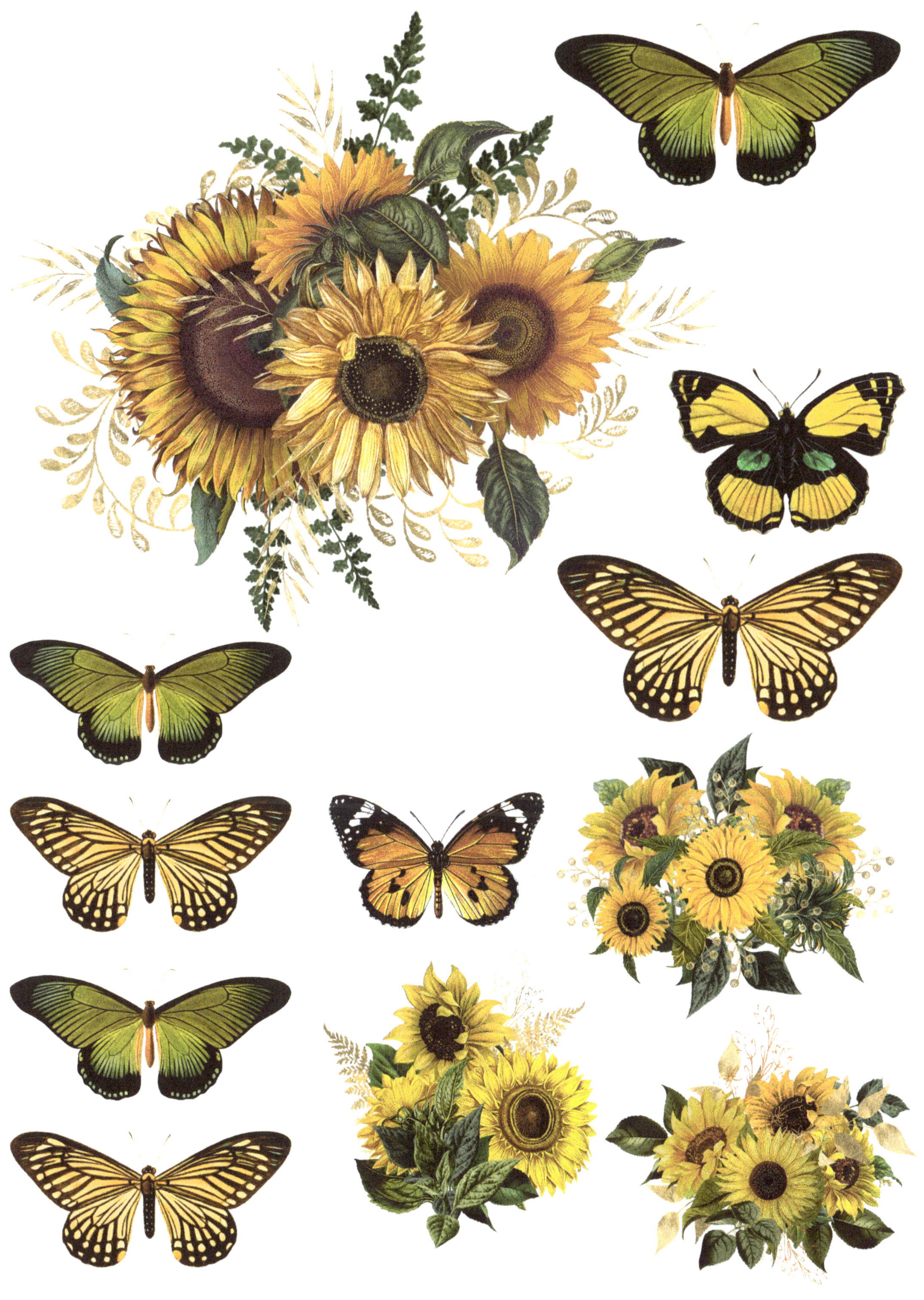

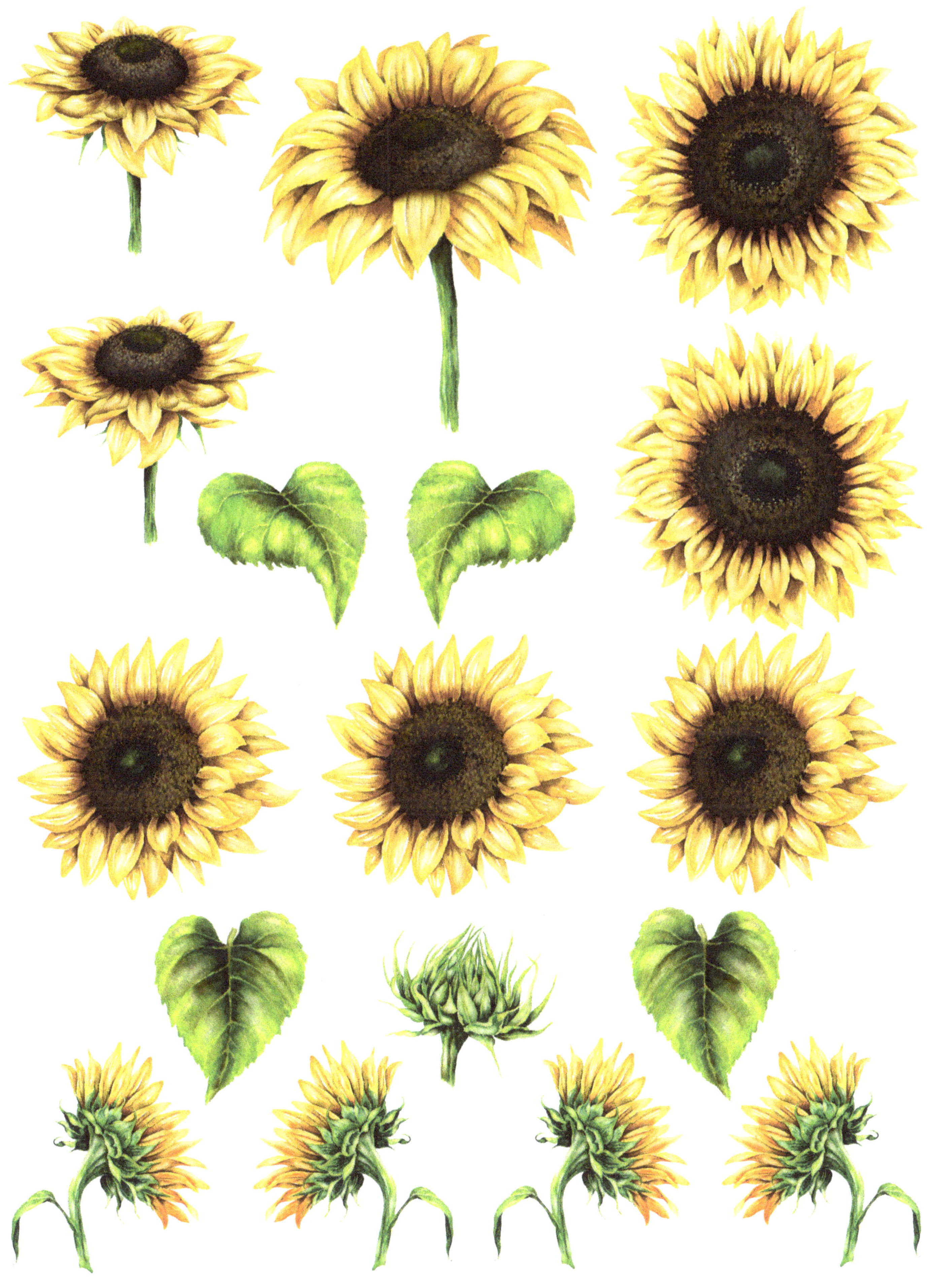

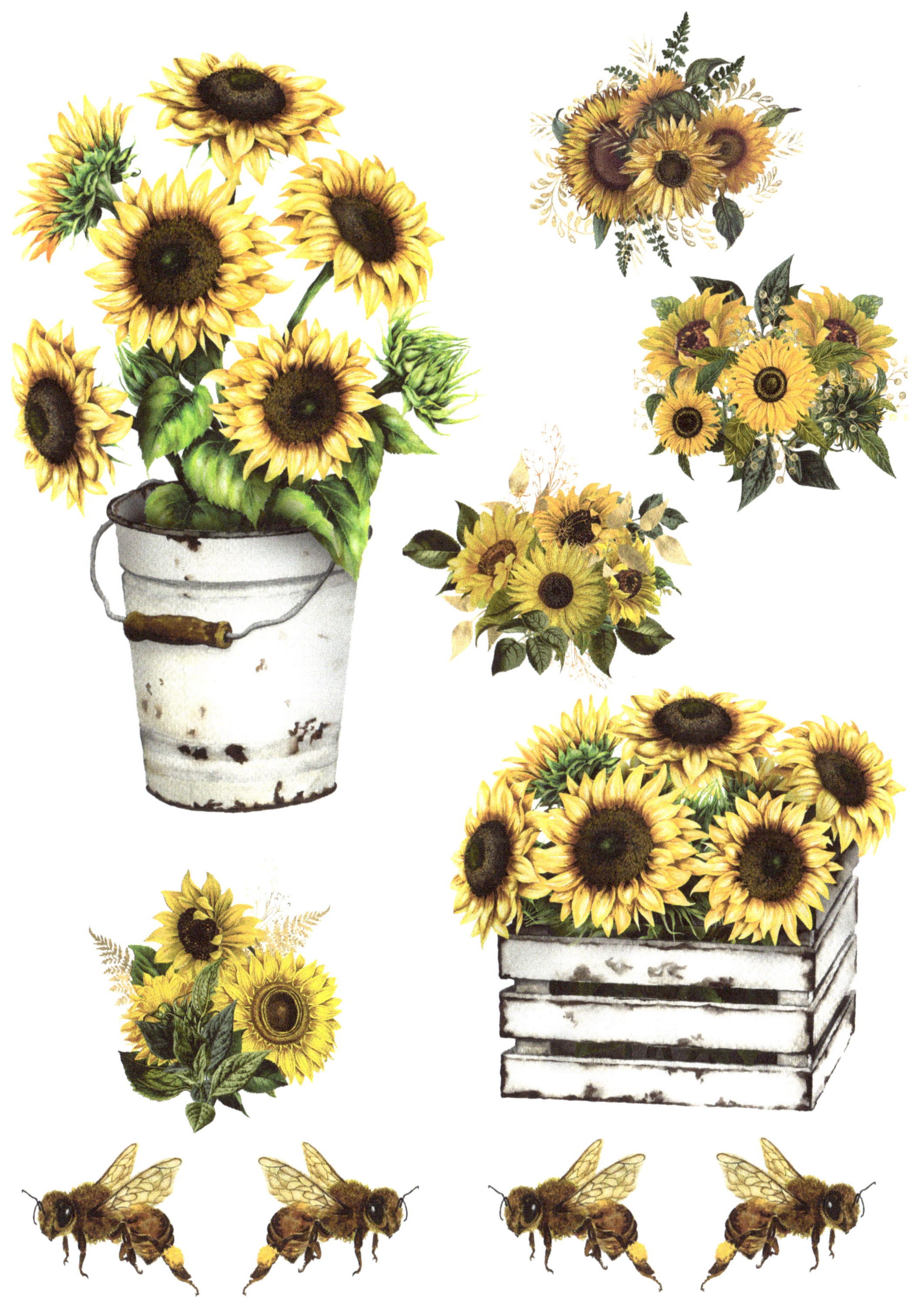

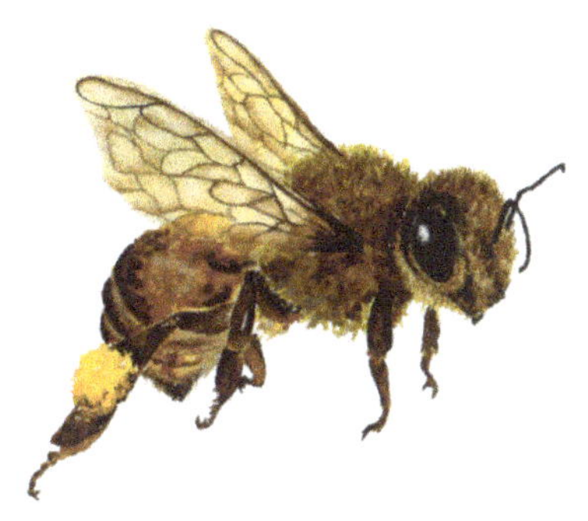

Dedicated to Your Artful Life from the Shiny Designs Studio.
www.ShinyDesigns.com

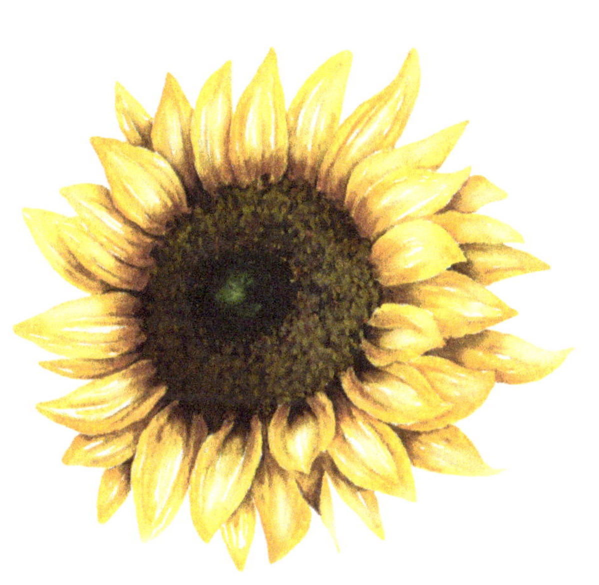
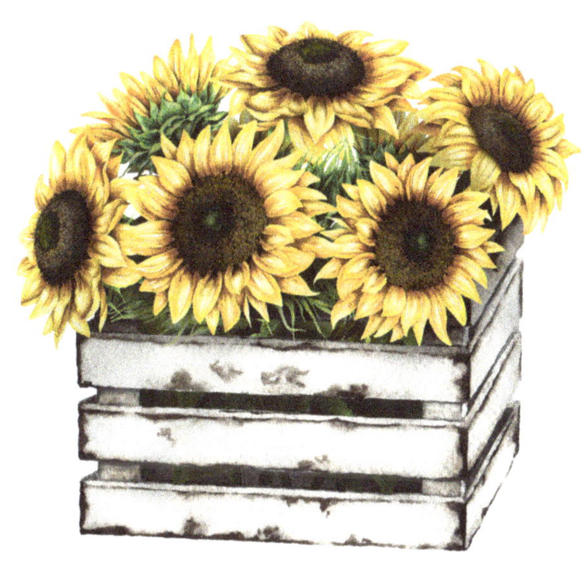
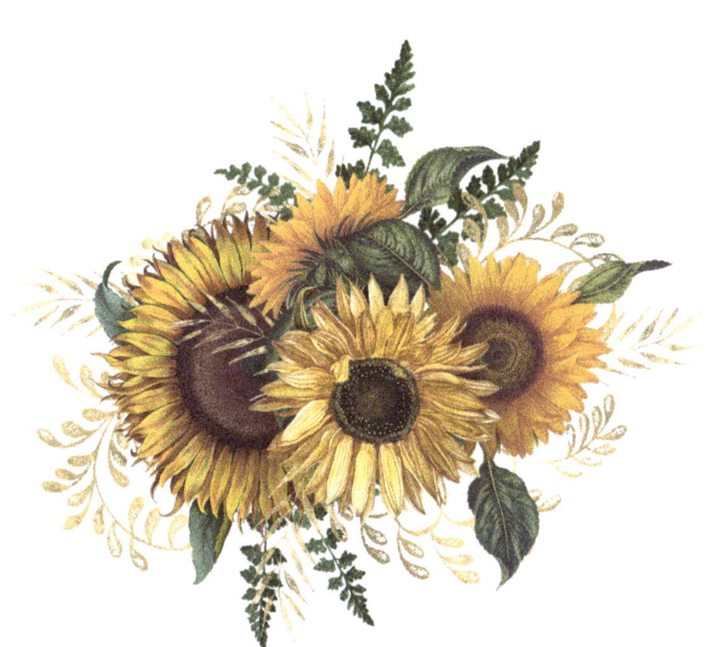
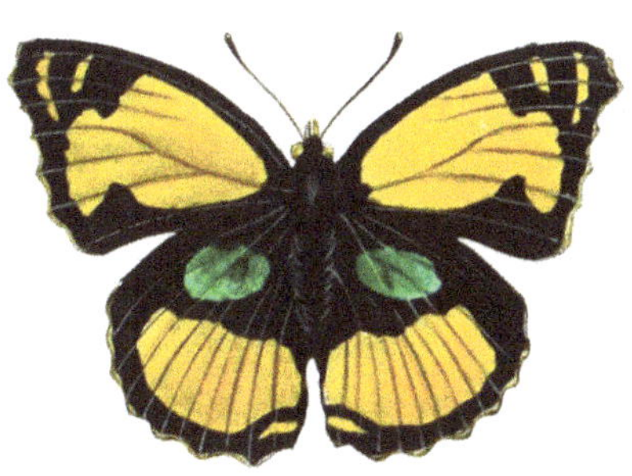

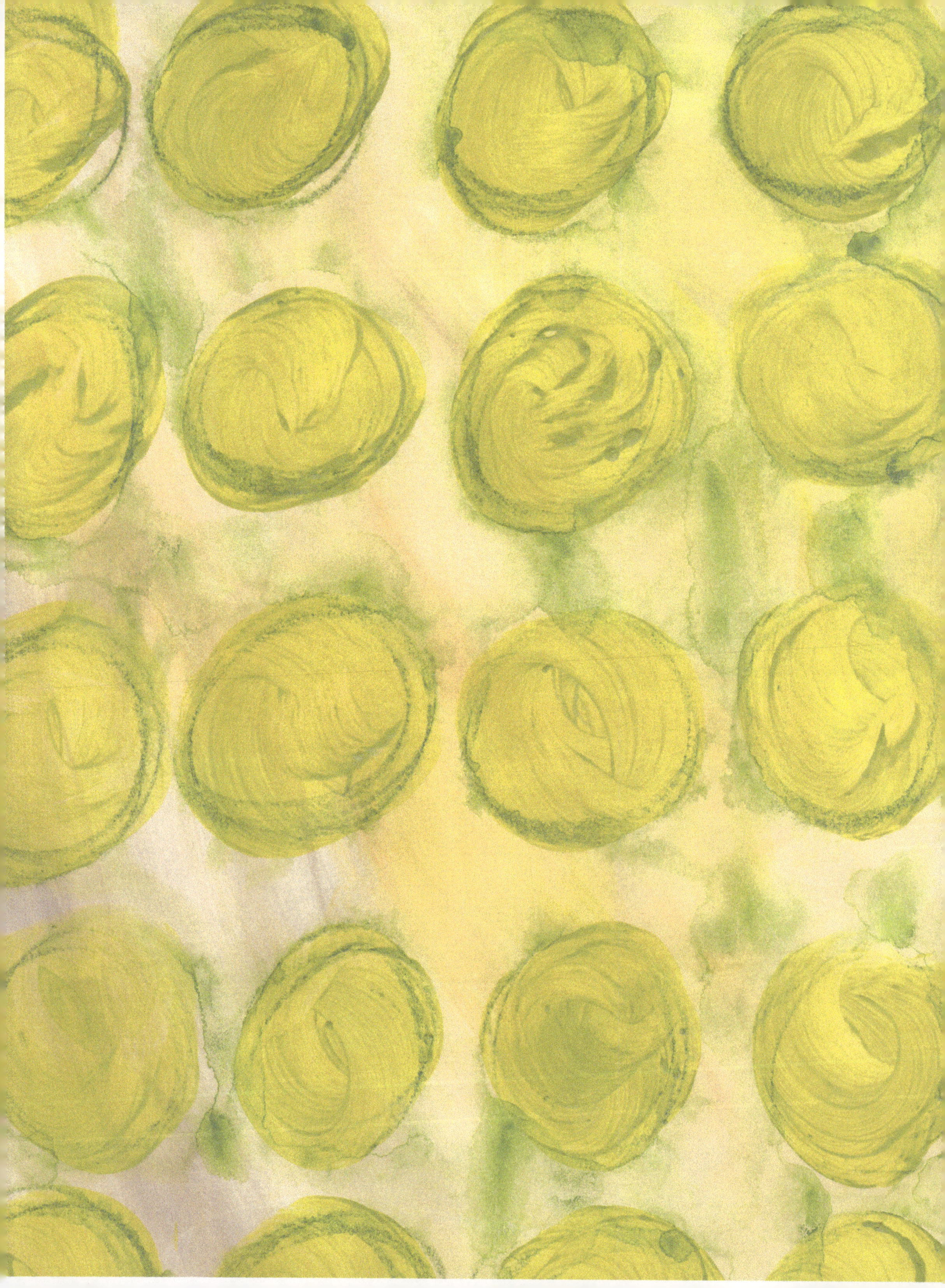